KU-300-818

Sleeping
ROUGH

Barbara Mitchelhill

Published in association with
The Basic Skills Agency

Hodder & Stoughton

A MEMBER OF THE HODDER HEADLINE GROUP

Acknowledgements
Cover: Louise Hilton/NB Illustration
Illustrations: Mike Bell

Orders: please contact Bookpoint Ltd, 130 Milton Park, Abingdon, Oxon OX14
4SB. Telephone: (44) 01235 827720, Fax: (44) 01235 400454. Lines are open from
9.00–6.00, Monday to Saturday, with a 24 hour message answering service. Email
address: orders@bookpoint.co.uk

British Library Cataloguing in Publication Data
A catalogue record for this title is available from The British Library

ISBN 0 340 86946 1

First published 1999
This edition published 2002
Impression number   10 9 8 7 6 5 4 3 2 1
Year   2007 2006 2005 2004 2003 2002

Copyright © 1999 Barbara Mitchelhill

Typeset by Fakenham Photosetting Ltd, Fakenham, Norfolk.
Printed in Great Britain for Hodder & Stoughton Educational, a division of
Hodder Headline Plc, 338 Euston Road, London NW1 3BH by Athenaeum Press,
Gateshead, Tyne & Wear.

About the play

The People
- Jed
- Pete

The Place
The middle of the countryside.

What's Happening
Pete and Jed have just got off a bus miles from anywhere to begin their camping weekend.

Pete   I never thought we'd get here.
That bus was dead old.
I didn't think it would make it
up that last hill.
Did you see that snail
trying to overtake us?

Jed   No.
I was too busy
watching that tortoise!

Pete   Yeah!
I didn't think it would take that long
to get here.
Still, those Australian kids
sitting behind us
were cool.
All that gear they had!
Amazing!

PUBLIC FOOTPATH

2

Jed   They were going walking
          further up the valley.
          To Hinton.
          The hills are steeper there.
          They must be really keen.

Pete   Help me on with my backpack,
          will you, Jed?
          It weighs a ton.

Jed   You're kidding.
          Mine's dead easy to carry.
          You're getting weak and feeble
          in your old age.

Pete   Oh yeah, yeah!
          Just give us a hand, will you
          – or we'll never get moving.

*Jed helps **Pete** on with his backpack.*

Jed How's that?

Pete Thanks.

That's OK.

Now we can get started.

We'll walk 'til it starts to get dark
and then we'll pitch the tent.

Jed Right.

Head for the hills!

Later that day,
the boys are miles from anywhere
and the light is fading.

Pete Cor! We've gone miles.

I can't walk much further.

I feel as if I've got the world
on my back.

Let's pack it in for today.

Jed   All right.
         If you want to.
         Let's stop here.
         It's nice and flat.
         No stones.
         No bumps.

         They slip off their backpacks.

Pete   Let's pitch the tent
         before it gets really dark.
         We can always eat our sandwiches later
         – if we don't fall asleep first.

Jed   Right.

I'll get the tent out then.

He tips the contents of his backpack
on to the ground.

What the …?

Pete   What's all that?

Jed   I don't know.

I didn't pack 'em.

They're not my clothes.

Pete   Well, where's the tent, Jed?

What have you done with it?

It was in there when we left home.

Jed   I know! I know!

I'm trying to think.

Pete   No wonder

you weren't complaining

about that backpack.

It only had T-shirts and jeans in it.

What happened to yours, then?

Jed   I must have left it on the bus.

Those Australian kids

– they had backpacks.

I put mine on the luggage rack

next to theirs.

They all look pretty much the same,

you must admit.

Pete   So you picked up the wrong one,
         did you?

Jed   Er ... yeah.
         I must have done.

Pete   Trust you!
         We'll have to report it
         to the police tomorrow.
         Maybe we'll get yours back sometime.

Jed   But what about tonight?

Pete   We'll have to sleep rough.
         There's nothing else to do out here.
         Look – there's a big oak
         on the other side of that hedge.
         We'll sleep under that.
         At least the weather's good.

They climb over the hedge
and settle down to sleep under the tree.

Jed   Pete! Pete!
      Wake up!
Pete What ...?
      What is it, Jed?
Jed   I can hear a funny noise.
Pete What kind of funny noise?
Jed   I dunno but it's getting nearer.
Pete Shhh!

Pause

I think I can hear it, too.

Pause

I think it's some kind of animal.

Jed   What kind?

Pete Something big.

Pause

Jed   **Wow! Help!**

You're right, Pete!

Look! Over there!

I can see it!

It's massive!

It's a bull

– and it's coming towards us.

Pete Don't sit there – get moving!
Run for it!

Jed I'm going! I'm going.

Pete Not that way, Jed.
Over here.
Come on!
Make for the hedge.

They run and scramble over the fence.

Pete Phew! We made it!
Are you OK?

Jed   (*panting*)
I think so.
I thought it was going to get me.
It was a real brute.
We got out just in time.

Pete   I've managed to grab my backpack.

Jed   I didn't.
I just ran.

Pete   It's a good thing
I've got the food in mine.
At least we won't starve tomorrow.
Come on over here, Jed.
It's OK by the hedge.
There's some nice thick grass.

Jed   Yeah! It looks all right.
Mmm. Quite comfy really.
It's a bit of an adventure
– sleeping rough.

Pete   It's going to be light soon.
Let's get some sleep.
I'm shattered
after lugging that backpack.

Jed   Pass it to me
before you nod off, will you?

Pete   What for?

Jed   I'm starving
and I feel like something to eat.

Pete passes the backpack.

Pete   You go ahead, if you want to.
I don't care
as long as I can get some sleep.

Jed   Aren't you hungry?

Pete   No!

*Pete falls asleep
while Jed searches in the bag for food.*

Jed Oh well,
I'll have to have the baked beans
to myself, then.
Where are they …?
Got 'em.
Now the tin opener … Yes!
Matches … pan … gas cooker.
Right!

He strikes a match.

Jed **OUCH! OUCH! OUCH!**
Pete What's the matter now?
Jed I was trying to light the cooker.
I burned my finger on the match.
Pete Trying to light the cooker?
You're crazy.
Why don't you have a bag of crisps
or something.
You can't cook at this time of night.

Jed   Why not?

I want something hot.

I'm cold and I'm hungry.

Pete   Forget it!

Go to sleep, Jed.

It'll soon be morning.

You're going to be tired out.

Now lie down.

Jed   But ...

Pete   Not another word.

GO TO SLEEP!

*Jed lies down next to Pete
and closes his eyes.*

Jed   Pete!

Pause

Pete!

Pause

Pete!

Pete sits up suddenly.

Pete What ... what ... what?
Jed A smell!
Pete What smell?
I can't smell anything?
I think you're ...

He sniffs.

Oh, I can!
I can smell something burning!

They both jump to their feet.

Jed   Over there.

The grass is on fire.

The match must have done it.

I dropped it, didn't I?

What can we do, Pete?

What can we do?

Pete   Take your T-shirt off.

Beat the flames.

Come on!

MOVE!

They begin to beat the flames
with their shirts.

Jed   Out! Out! Out!

I'll beat you to death.

Die you devils. Die!

Pete   Keep at it, Jed.

If the fire reaches the hedge,
we've had it.

It'll spread like crazy.

They carry on beating
until the flames die out.

Jed   Cor! I'm done in.
         I've never worked so hard
         in all my life.
         I never thought we'd put it out.

Pete I know.
         I was dead scared.
         The flames could have spread
         right across the hillside.

Jed   Huh! Just look at my T-shirt.
         It's black!

Pete You mean, what's left of it.
         There are more holes than T-shirt.

Jed   I don't know
         what Mum's going to say about it.

Pete I do!
         She'll go mad!
         It was brand new.

Jed   Oh well.
         I can't think about that now.

Let's get some sleep.

They lie down again.

Jed	Pete.
Pete	Yeah?
Jed	Did you feel something just then?
Pete	What?
Jed	A spot of rain.
	I think it's going to pour down.
	I think I can hear thunder, too.
Pete	(*sitting up*)
	I don't believe it!
	I don't believe it!
	We've lost our tent.
	We've had the bull and the fire.
	Nothing else can go wrong, can it?
Jed	I think it can, Pete.
	I think we're going to get very wet.

Thunder rumbles in the distance.
Rain begins to fall

and lightning flashes.

Pete You're right, Jed.
And we'll just have to sit here
like a pair of dummies 'til it stops.

Jed I bet those Australians
think we have rotten weather
in this country.
They're not used to getting wet
when they go camping.

Pete I don't suppose they know it's raining.
They're probably fast asleep
in their tent!
In fact, they might be sleeping
in our tent!
That must be nice for them
– extra room.

Jed Well, there's only one thing to say, Pete.
We might be getting soaking wet,
but I bet the Australians are grateful!